Walking Down the Corridor of

HOLY WEEK

— to Easter Day —

The Venerable

Alson B. H. Percival, Ph.D.

To Margaret, my beloved wife and faithful companion, thank you for your patience, your sacrifice, and your unwavering support. This work is as much yours as it is mine.

REJOICE GREATLY, O DAUGHTER OF ZION! SHOUT ALOUD,
O DAUGHTER OF JERUSALEM! BEHOLD, YOUR KING IS
COMING TO YOU." — ZECHARIAH 9:9

Table of Contents

Walking Through Holy Week

FOREWORD

Holy Week is a short discourse by Alson B H Percival, Ph.D

It highlights and emphasizes the events concerning the week of passion of our Lord, the week between Palm Sunday, the day Jesus rode into Jerusalem midst shouts of Hosanna, "Save Now," and just five days later when roughly the same people shouted, "Crucify Him."

On Palm Sunday, they threw their palms and themselves at His feet; on Good Friday, they were screaming for His blood.

If God wanted to demonstrate to us, the world, what mercurial, unreliable hypocrites we are, there could be no better way to show us.

In this short survey, Dr. Percival has outlined for us the day-by-day events, the highs and lows, the agony of those terrible days between Palm Sunday and Good Friday, when the innocent suffered for the guilty, when Christ paid the price in blood for our shame. For indeed it is written, "And almost all things are by the law purged with blood; and without shedding of blood, there is no remission." (Hebrews 9:22).

But behold, as was the agony, so also was the ecstasy, that glorious Resurrection Morning, when the angel proclaimed, "He is not here; He is risen, Alleluia, He is risen, Alleluia, Alleluia!"

~ John S. Weekes, B. A. Law, Th. D. Rel. Ed. D. ~

INTRODUCTION
Walk-Through Holy Week

What is Holy Week?

Holy Week (Palm Sunday to Easter) is the most sacred eight-day Christian observance, commemorating the Passion, death, and resurrection of Jesus Christ and marking the culmination of Lent. It commemorates the final days of Christ's earthly ministry, from His triumphal entry to His resurrection, highlighting His ultimate sacrifice for humanity. While Holy Week is a focused period of remembrance, the call to holiness is not bound by time. God commands His people: "Speak to all the congregation of the people of Israel and say to them, you shall be holy, for I the LORD your God am holy" (Leviticus 19:2; see also Exodus 19:6). The apostle Peter echoes this call, writing, "Be holy because I am holy" (1 Peter 1:16).

The Significance of Holy Week

Holy Week memorializes the character of Jesus' final days on Earth. Out of love for humanity, Jesus endured the cruel punishment reserved for the worst criminals of His time. In doing so, He fulfilled the prophecy given through Isaiah, who foresaw the Messiah's suffering as the path to humanity's salvation (Isaiah 52–53).

The liturgical observance of Holy Week includes the following days:
- **Palm Sunday**: Jesus' triumphant entry into Jerusalem, welcomed by crowds with palm branches.
- **Holy Monday**: Jesus began His journey from Bethany to Jerusalem and taught along the way.
- **Holy Tuesday**: Jesus returned to Jerusalem, confronting religious authorities and sharing parables and other teachings.

- **Holy Wednesday:** Often referred to as "Spy Wednesday." This day commemorates Judas Iscariot's betrayal of Jesus for thirty pieces of silver.
- **Holy Thursday (Maundy Thursday):** Jesus instituted the Holy Eucharist, the ministry of foot-washing, and the New Law of Love.
- **Good Friday:** Also known as Holy Friday, this day commemorates Jesus' crucifixion, death, and burial.
- **Holy Saturday:** Jesus remained in the tomb, a day of quiet reflection and anticipation.
- **Easter Sunday:** Resurrection Day, when Jesus rose from the dead at dawn, inaugurating the New Covenant promised in Jeremiah 31:31–34.
- **Easter Monday:** A day of joy and renewal within the Easter Octave, extending the Resurrection celebration and the victory of salvation.

Most scholars, including some from the Journal of the Evangelical Theological Society (JETS), recognize Holy Week as a profound period of reflection, renewal, and sacrifice, serving as a cornerstone of faith that commemorates the Passion, death, and resurrection of Jesus. It is described as a beacon of hope and an opportunity for believers to engage in acts of service, deepen their connection to the community, and return to God.

HOLY WEEK

*A devotional journey
from Palm Sunday to Easter Day*

PALM SUNDAY
THE TRIUMPHAL ENTRY AND
THE JOURNEY TOWARD CALVARY

Opening Prayer

Almighty and ever-living Lord Jesus Christ, as You set Your face toward Jerusalem and the cross that awaits You, grant us grace to follow where You lead. Order our hearts in obedience, deepen our faith, and draw us into the mystery of Your redeeming love, who lives and reigns with the Father and the Holy Spirit, one God, now and forever. Amen.

Scripture Reading: Luke 2:39–52

Reflection

The Gospel according to Saint Luke grants the Church a rare and illuminating glimpse into Jesus' early self-awareness of His divine vocation. At the age of twelve, during a Passover pilgrimage to Jerusalem, Jesus remained behind in the Temple while His parents began the journey home. After three days, one day's travel out, one day returning, and a third spent searching in the city, Mary and Joseph found Him seated among the teachers of the Law, listening attentively and engaging them with questions. All who heard Him were amazed at His understanding and His answers (Luke 2:46–47).

This moment marks the first recorded instance in which Jesus openly identifies Himself with the will and purpose of His heavenly Father. His response to Mary, "Did you know that I must be in my Father's house" (or, following the older rendering, "about my Father's business"; Luke 2:49), reveals a conscious and obedient alignment with the mission entrusted to Him.

His presence among those charged with teaching and guarding the Law stands as a profound disclosure of His identity and vocation. This episode should not be read through the lens of a later Bar Mitzvah ceremony; Luke frames it theologically as a Christological declaration rather than merely a rite of passage.

Following this episode, the Gospel narrative enters a season of holy silence. When Jesus emerged publicly at approximately thirty years of age (Luke 3:23), He was first baptized by John in the Jordan and then began His Galilean ministry in the power of the Spirit (Luke 3:19–20; cf. Matt 4:12; Mark 1:14). John's death at the hands of Herod (Luke 9:7–9; Matt 14:1–12) came during the course of that ministry, not before its commencement. From that point, Jesus proclaimed the Kingdom of God through word and deed, declaring at Nazareth the fulfillment of the Isaianic promise (Luke 4:14–21; cf. Isa 61:1–2).

Palm Sunday commemorates the climax of this ministry: Jesus' deliberate, prophetically laden entry into Jerusalem. Riding upon an unridden colt, itself a sign of royal and sacred consecration, He descends the Mount of Olives as the crowds spread their cloaks upon the road and cry out, "Blessed is the King who comes in the name of the Lord! Peace in heaven and glory in the highest!" (Luke 19:38; cf. Ps 118:26). Matthew and John record the explicit fulfillment of Zechariah 9:9, which says, "Rejoice greatly, Daughter Zion! Shout, Daughter Jerusalem! See, your king comes to you, righteous and victorious, lowly and riding on a donkey, on a colt, the foal of a donkey," underscoring that this entry is not an improvised popular movement but a deliberately enacted messianic sign.

The observance of Holy Week points to the broader narrative of salvation. After His resurrection, Jesus ascended to rejoin the Father, where He intercedes for His Church and prepares a place for believers (John 14:2–3).[4] While He waits in heaven, His return is imminent, and Christians remain watchful for the rapture of the Church before the Tribulation (Matthew 24:36; 1 Thessalonians 4:16, 18). As we journey through Holy Week, our focus is on Christ's ultimate sacrifice and victorious resurrection, reminding us of God's unwavering love, the call to holiness, and the hope of eternal life.

Closing Prayer

Dear Jesus, whether I walk through the valley of death or await the final gathering of Your Church, grant that I may remain with You forever. Let Your presence be my comfort and my guide, and may I trust in the triumph of Your resurrection. Amen.

Footnotes

1. Luke 2:46–47: The "three days" likely represent one day traveling out, one day returning, and one day searching; in the Temple, Jesus engaged in the rabbinical tradition of question-and-answer, showcasing divine understanding; see BibleStudy.com "The Boy Jesus in the Temple" (1.2.4).
2. Luke 2:49: The Greek phrase en tois tou patros mou is ambiguous, allowing translations of either "in my Father's house" (referring to the Temple) or "about my Father's business" (referring to his mission), with many modern translations opting for the former, but both emphasizing his divine consciousness; see Zondervan Academic "Father's house or business" (1.4.5).
3. Divine Vocation/Alignment: The usage of "must" (Greek: dei) indicates a divine necessity or obligation, signaling that Jesus was already operating under the mandate of his mission; see BibleHub "What does Jesus mean by 'in My Father's house'" (1.3.3).

4. Bar Mitzvah vs. Theological Narrative: While sometimes associated with the Jewish age of accountability, scholars emphasize that Luke presents this incident to demonstrate Jesus' early, unique, and conscious alignment with God, rather than a mere cultural rite; see Stack Exchange "Was there some significance to the mention of Jesus' age in Lk 2:42" (1.5.1).
5. Ministry Timeline: Luke records the ministry beginning around age thirty, following his baptism and the imprisonment of John, with John's execution occurring later in the narrative (Luke 9:7–9). See BibleStudy.com "The Boy Jesus in the Temple" (1.2.6).
6. Fulfilment of Prophecy: Jesus' declaration at Nazareth (Luke 4:14–21) explicitly connects his ministry to Isaiah 61, identifying himself as the bringer of the Kingdom of God; see BibleStudy.com "The Boy Jesus in the Temple" (1.2.6).
7. Palm Sunday/Climax: The culmination of this ministry occurs in Jerusalem, where Jesus consciously fulfils prophecy; see BibleHub "What does Jesus mean by 'in My Father's house'" (1.3.3)

Holy Monday

Jesus in the Temple

Opening Prayer

Lord Christ, we desire to follow Your example in faithful obedience to Your Father. Lead us as we journey toward You, that Your truth and humility may form our hearts. Amen.

Scripture Reading: Gospel of Matthew 21:23–27

Reflection

On Holy Monday, the Church contemplates Christ's return to Jerusalem and the unfolding of the second decisive phase of His redemptive mission. In the Gospel of Matthew, the Evangelist presents Jesus exercising divine authority in both word and action. The religious leaders question His authority, yet His response reveals the spiritual blindness that has overtaken those entrusted with the care of Israel's worship.

Within this broader narrative, the Synoptic tradition records two prophetic signs: the cursing of the fig tree and the cleansing of the Temple. These actions are not merely emotional reactions but deliberate, symbolic judgments. The Temple, consecrated as the dwelling place of Almighty God, had become a centre of outward religiosity devoid of inward devotion. Likewise, the fig tree, outwardly promising fruit yet barren, becomes a living parable of spiritual sterility.

Jesus' grief arises from a deeper concern. The leaders and many among the people have ceased to regard God as the true centre of their life and worship. Ritual continues, yet reverence has diminished.

Knowledge of God persists in form, but it has grown distant and superficial in substance. The tragedy is not the absence of ceremony, but the absence of living faith.

The imagery of the fig tree carries rich prophetic significance. In Micah 4:4, the prophet envisions the Messianic age as a time of peace, when each person rests securely beneath the vine and fig tree. The barrenness Christ encountered stands in sharp contrast to that promise. It becomes a sign of Israel's failure to recognize and receive her Messiah.

Similarly, the prophet Joel recalls the Lord's generous provision of grain, wine, and oil for His covenant people. However, abundance led to forgetfulness rather than gratitude. Through the call of the Book of Joel, Israel is summoned to repentance marked by sincerity, humility, and renewed trust in divine mercy. Repentance opens the way to restoration and covenant faithfulness.

In Jesus Christ, these prophetic warnings and promises converge. The deliverance He brings surpasses the memory of the exodus from Egypt. Through His death and resurrection, He inaugurates a greater redemption. The way of the cross, though marked by sacrifice, becomes the path to life, peace, and enduring joy.

Holy Monday, therefore, calls believers to self-examination. It summons the Church to consider whether her worship bears fruit worthy of repentance, and whether her devotion reflects authentic love for God. Christ's cleansing of the Temple is not only a historical event but an abiding invitation to interior renewal.

Closing Prayer

Lord Jesus Christ, grant that we may walk faithfully in the way of the cross, trusting in Your saving love, and rejoicing in the peace that You alone can give. Amen.

Footnotes

1. Matthew 21:23–27: Jesus is questioned by the chief priests and elders regarding His authority to teach and cleanse the Temple, to which He responds by questioning them about the source of John the Baptist's baptism.
2. Matthew 21:23–27, 28–22:14 (Contextual Analysis): The leaders' refusal to answer shows their fear of the crowd and lack of spiritual integrity, leading to Jesus' judgment parables.
3. Matthew 21:12–17: Jesus drives out merchants and money changers, asserting divine authority as the True High Priest.
4. Mark 11:12–25: The fig tree incident is presented in Mark as a "sandwich" surrounding the cleansing of the Temple, acting as a sign of judgment on the religious system.
5. GotQuestions.org: "Why did Jesus curse the fig tree?" The fig tree represents Israel; fruitlessness indicates a lack of genuine salvation despite outward religious observance.
6. St. Paul Center: "What Has Jesus Got Against Fig Trees?" The fig tree symbolizes Israel, and the cursing points to its lack of fruit, mirroring the Temple's failure as a house of prayer (alluding to Jer 8:13).
7. The Bible Project: "Jesus on the Cursed Tree": Jesus links the fruitless tree with the corrupt Temple system, marking it for judgment.
8. "Why did Jesus curse the fig tree?" The barren tree is a symbol of Israel, and the cursing signals that the Kingdom is being taken from those who reject the Messiah.
9. "Cursing of the fig tree": The event is interpreted as a symbolic judgment against the Jewish leadership and a warning of impending destruction.
10. BibleHub.com: "How does Micah 4:4 relate to the concept of the Messianic age?" The vine and fig tree represent security and peace under the Messianic reign.
11. "Everyone Will Live In Peace…": The image of the vine and fig tree symbolizes the fulfillment of the covenant and the peace of the Millennial reign.

12. Joel 2:12–13: The Lord commands a return to Him with the heart, not just outward garments, emphasizing repentance.
13. Reformed Bible Studies: "The Call for Repentance": The locust plague symbolizes devastation from which God promises to restore His people if they truly repent.

HOLY TUESDAY

Opening Prayer

Lord Jesus Christ, You have set before us the perfect example of faithful obedience as You walk resolutely toward the cross. Grant us grace to follow in Your footsteps with steadfast hearts and willing spirits. Amen.

Scripture Reading: Colossians 1:15–20

Reflection

The apostle Paul proclaims Christ as the image of the invisible God, the firstborn of all creation, through whom all things are made and in whom all things hold together. In this passage, reconciliation stands at the very center of Christ's redemptive work. Through His blood shed on the cross, peace is made between God and a humanity estranged by sin, a reconciliation that flows entirely from divine initiative, as God in Christ draws the alienated world back to Himself (2 Cor 5:18–20; Col 1:20–22).

The immensity of this reconciling work did not overwhelm the Son. Rather, Christ advanced in perfect fidelity, step by step, in obedience to the Father's will, a pattern that gives shape and purpose to the events of Holy Tuesday. The theological vision of Colossians 1 thus furnishes the cosmic frame within which the particular incidents of this day must be read: the cursing of the barren fig tree, the extended debates in the Temple, and the sober eschatological discourse that follows.

On this day, traditionally associated with Jesus' extended teaching and controversial debates in the Temple, Jesus departs from Bethany and returns to Jerusalem. Encountering the barren fig tree, He employs it as a living parable to teach His disciples that God's people are called to genuine fruitfulness rather than outward show devoid of substance. Faith, repentance, and mission are the visible fruits of those who truly stand within the covenant community of God (Matt 21:18–22; Mark 11:12–14, 20–26).

Jesus continues to instruct His disciples, underscoring that the suffering He is about to endure, the wounds of the cross, and the shedding of His blood are not signs of defeat but acts of obedience to the Father's redemptive purpose. He calls His followers to take up their own crosses and follow Him (Matt 16:24; Mark 8:34; Luke 9:23; 14:27), assuring them that the one who endures to the end will be saved (Matt 24:13).

As the one who is at once Son of God (Col 1:13–15) and truly born of woman (Gal 4:4), the firstborn of all creation and the firstborn from the dead (Col 1:15, 18), Jesus revealed a way of life rooted in faithful community and moral integrity. He warns His followers not to imitate those who distort God's purposes through injustice or hypocrisy (Matt 23:1–36; Luke 20:45–47). Instead, they are sent forth to proclaim that the kingdom of God is near, calling others to repentance, faith, and renewed obedience, as reflected in His extended teachings recorded in Matthew's Gospel.

On this Holy Tuesday, we are invited to consider what it means to bear fruit worthy of the kingdom. The barren fig tree stands as a warning against a religion of form without substance.

However, the same Lord who condemns barrenness also opens, through His cross, the way of reconciliation and new life. We are called, in the light of Colossians 1, to trust that the God who holds all creation together in His Son is also holding together our own fragmented lives, and to walk, step by step, in obedient love.

Closing Prayer

Lord Jesus Christ, the wounds You bore upon the cross run deep, yet they bring healing and reconciliation to the world. Grant us patience and courage to walk faithfully on the road of discipleship, step by step, trusting in Your strength and grace. Amen.

Footnotes

1. Colossians 1:15–17: This passage establishes Christ's preeminence in creation, identifying Him as the eikŏn (image) of the invisible God and the sustainer of the cosmos.
2. Colossians 1:20: Paul asserts that God was pleased to reconcile all things to Himself through Christ, specifically through the "blood of His cross."
3. 2 Corinthians 5:18–20: Paul emphasizes that this reconciliation is a "divine initiative," stating that "all this is from God, who reconciled us to Himself through Christ."
4. Philippians 2:8: Christ's "perfect fidelity" is seen in His humbling of Himself and becoming "obedient to death—even death on a cross."
5. Matthew 21–25: These chapters outline the specific events of Holy Tuesday, including the fig tree (21:18–22), Temple debates (21:23–23:39), and the Olivet Discourse (24–25).
6. Mark 11:12, 20: The chronological markers in Mark's Gospel record Jesus traveling from Bethany back to Jerusalem on the days following the Triumphal Entry.
7. Matthew 21:19: The cursing of the fig tree is widely interpreted as a symbolic judgment on religious hypocrisy and the lack of spiritual fruit.
8. Mark 11:22–25: Jesus explicitly connects the lesson of the withered tree to the necessity of faith and forgiveness in the life of the disciple.

9. Hebrews 12:2: Christ endured the cross "for the joy set before him," viewing the suffering as the path to redemptive victory.
10. Matthew 24:13: Within the eschatological context of Holy Tuesday's teaching, Jesus promises salvation to those who remain faithful through trials.

HOLY WEDNESDAY

Opening Prayer

Almighty and ever-living God, as we enter the solemn stillness of Holy Wednesday, quiet our hearts before You. Draw us into deeper communion with Your Son, who remained faithful in prayer and obedience even as betrayal drew near. Grant us grace to watch and pray, to discern truth from deception, and to walk faithfully in the way of the Cross. Through Jesus Christ our Lord. Amen.

Scripture Reading: Matthew 26:6–13; 26:14–25; 27:3–10 | Mark 14:3–9 | Luke 22:1–6

Reflection

Holy Wednesday stands at the threshold between Jesus' public ministry and the events of His Passion. The Gospel accounts situate the final days of Jesus' earthly life in a rhythm of Temple teaching by day and prayerful withdrawal to the Mount of Olives by night (Luke 21:37–38). This pattern of public witness and private communion with the Father shapes the character of the entire week, and Wednesday draws particular attention to two contrasting figures whose actions decisively shape the Passion narrative: the unnamed woman who anoints Jesus, and Judas Iscariot, who betrays Him.

The anointing of Jesus at Bethany is recounted in Matthew and Mark immediately before the account of Judas's negotiations with the chief priests, and this juxtaposition appears deliberate.

The aftermath of Judas's act is recounted in Matthew 27:3–10, where, seized with remorse upon learning that Jesus had been condemned, he returns the thirty pieces of silver and takes his own life. The chief priests, unwilling to return the money to the treasury as it is blood money, use it to purchase the potter's field as a burial place for foreigners, an ironic fulfillment of the prophetic word, and a reminder that Judas's gain was accompanied by irreversible loss. Scripture presents his story not for mere condemnation, but as a sobering account of the cost of choosing expediency over faithfulness, money over friendship, and self-interest over the call to follow.

However, Judas's failure does not divert Jesus from His purpose. Throughout these events, Jesus remains the obedient Son, wholly committed to the Father's redemptive will (John 5:19; Heb 5:8). The betrayal, the anointing, and the gathering shadow of the Passion all converge toward the Cross, where the purpose of the Incarnation reaches its appointed fulfilment (Isa 53:10–11).

Holy Wednesday presents the Church with two contrasting responses to Christ: costly devotion and calculated betrayal. The anonymous woman of Bethany offers all she has without reserve; Judas calculates what he might gain. Jesus receives her act as love; the evangelists describe his in terms of satanic agency and tragic loss. The day, therefore, calls believers to examine the quality of their own allegiance, whether their following of Christ is marked by genuine self-giving or by a discipleship that remains conditional, measured, and self-serving.

The silence and stillness of Holy Wednesday, a day with no formal liturgical commemoration in most Western rites, is itself instructive. It invites a posture of watchfulness and interior preparation, consonant with the call to prayer and vigilance that Jesus would issue to His disciples in Gethsemane (Matt 26:41; Mark 14:38; Luke 22:46). In this sense, Holy Wednesday is not merely a commemoration of past events but a call to the Church in every age: to remain awake, to discern faithfully, and to receive Christ with the costly and unhesitating devotion exemplified by the woman who anointed Him for burial.

Closing Prayer

Lord Jesus Christ, we give thanks for all who have loved You with wholehearted devotion, and we are sobered by the account of those who have turned away. Grant us hearts of faithful love, steadfast obedience, and sincere repentance. Keep us loyal to You in all things, that we may follow the way of the Cross with courage and trust, and lead others into the fullness of Your saving grace. Amen.

Footnotes

1. Exodus 21:32 stipulates that thirty shekels of silver was the standard compensation to an enslaved person's owner if the enslaved person was gored to death by an ox, highlighting the low valuation placed on Jesus by the authorities.
2. Zechariah 11:12–13 describes the prophet being paid thirty pieces of silver for his work as a shepherd, a "handsome price" in sarcastic terms, which God instructs him to throw to the potter, symbolizing the rejection of the true Shepherd.

HOLY THURSDAY

MAUNDY THURSDAY

Opening Prayer

We offer praise, honor, and glory to You, Lord, for Your humility made manifest in the New Commandment and in the institution of the Holy Eucharist, gifts by which believers are drawn toward the eternal dwelling You are preparing. Amen.

Scripture Reading: John 13:31–38 (NRSV)

Reflection

The designation "Maundy Thursday" derives from the Latin term Mandatum, meaning "commandment", a word drawn directly from Jesus' proclamation: "A new commandment I give to you" (John 13:34). The term thus anchors the day's observance firmly in the dominical imperative that defines its theological character.

Within popular Christian culture, Maundy Thursday has historically been associated with domestic preparations for the Good Friday fast. Among the most enduring of these traditions is the baking of Hot Cross Buns, whose cruciform markings serve as edible symbols of the Passion. The vendor's street cry, "Hot Cross Buns, one a penny, two a penny", has documented origins in eighteenth-century England and reflects the interweaving of liturgical commemoration with the rhythms of everyday life.

The liturgical significance of Maundy Thursday is traditionally understood to encompass three distinct but theologically interrelated gifts bestowed by Christ upon His disciples:

1. The Institution of the Holy Eucharist. The Last Supper, as narrated in the Synoptic Gospels and interpreted in light of John's account, constitutes the founding event of the sacrament of Holy Communion, through which the Church perpetually commemorates Christ's sacrificial self-offering.

2. The Paradigm of Servant Leadership. The act of Jesus washing His disciples' feet (John 13:1–17) establishes a Christological model of humble service that subverts conventional hierarchies of power and authority.

3. The New Commandment. The injunction to love one another as Christ has loved, "Just as I have loved you, you also should love one another" (John 13:34), both reaffirms and reconfigures the Mosaic double commandment of love, grounding it in the unprecedented standard of Christ's own self-giving love.

The Johannine passion narrative simultaneously foregrounds the reality of human moral failure. Jesus, perceiving the duplicitous intent of Judas Iscariot, discloses that one among the Twelve would betray Him (John 13:21–26). The evangelist's notation that "it was night" (John 13:30) upon Judas's departure carries both temporal and symbolic significance, evoking the Johannine theme of darkness as a figure for spiritual alienation. Similarly, Jesus forewarns Peter that he will deny knowing Him three times before the rooster crows (John 13:36–38), a prediction that anticipates the disciples' collective failure to grasp the full weight of the events about to unfold.

One scholar has observed that a guilty conscience frequently conceals itself behind explicit verbal disavowal—the protestation "I did not do this deed"—while covertly executing its premeditated course of action. This dynamic is powerfully illustrated in Judas, who departs to orchestrate the arrest of Jesus in the Garden of Gethsemane, and in Peter, whose impulsive defense of Jesus—striking the ear of the high priest's servant (John 18:10)—ultimately precedes his threefold denial. These narratives of betrayal and denial serve a crucial theological function: they underscore the radical grace by which Christ initiates the redemptive work that would be definitively realized through His resurrection.

Closing Prayer

We give thanks, Lord, for the gifts that renew and commission us for Your service. Amen.

Footnotes

1. "Maundy Thursday," Wikipedia, accessed February 28, 2026, https://en.wikipedia.org/wiki/Maundy_Thursday
2. "What is Maundy Thursday / Holy Thursday?" GotQuestions.org, accessed February 28, 2026, https://www.gotquestions.org/Maundy-Thursday.html
3. "Hot Cross Buns: The Ancient Story Behind Easter's Favorite Bread," azpieguys.com, accessed February 28, 2026, https://azpieguys.com/2025/03/24/hot-cross-buns-the-ancient-story-behind-easters-favorite-bread/
4. "Holy or heretical? A history of hot cross buns," English Heritage, accessed February 28, 2026, https://www.english-heritage.org.uk/easter/a-history-of-hot-cross-buns/
5. "Maundy Thursday: A Day Of Complex Religious Significance," The Space, accessed February 28, 2026, https://thespace.ink/essays/maundy-thursday-a-day-of-complex-religious-significance/

GOOD FRIDAY
THE PASSION OF OUR LORD

Opening Prayer

Almighty and everlasting God, on this day Your Son endured the pains of the cross for our redemption. Grant that we may receive the benefits of His suffering and death and follow Him with steadfast hearts in the way of obedience and love. Amen.

Scripture Reading: John 19:31–42

Reflection

On this solemn day, the true kingship of our Lord Jesus Christ is subjected to its supreme test. The world witnesses the Son of God enduring the lowest depths of human suffering, yet behind the scenes, the Father is fulfilling His divine purpose. This reminds us that God's will is accomplished through both obedience and suffering, a pattern declared in the Son's own words: "The Son can do nothing of His own accord, but only what He sees the Father doing" (John 5:19), and expounded by the apostolic witness: "Although He was a Son, He learned obedience through what He suffered" (Heb 5:8).

Jesus's passion reveals the full weight of human cruelty. He becomes the Rock of Salvation, typified in the Old Testament experiences of Moses at Horeb (Exodus 17:1–7; Num 20:10–12; 1 Cor 10:4). Unlike Moses, who strikes the rock in anger and thereby forfeits entry into the Promised Land (Num 20:12), Christ endures mockery, scourging, a crown of thorns, and every form of physical abuse, remaining wholly obedient to His Father's will precisely where Moses failed.

Even in His thirst, He is tormented, fulfilling the messianic lament: "For My thirst they gave Me vinegar to drink" (Ps 69:21 [LXX 68:22]). In His cry from the cross (Ps 22:1; cf. Matt 27:46; Mark 15:34), He demonstrates not despair but the unwavering trust of the righteous sufferer, calling upon the Father rather than earthly deliverance. In complete surrender, He commits His spirit into the Father's hands (Ps 31:5; Luke 23:46).

Though buried on the day of His death, His obedience is vindicated. The tearing of the temple curtain (Matt 27:51; Mark 15:38; Luke 23:45) signifies that access to God's presence has been opened by His atoning sacrifice (cf. Heb 10:19–20), while the resurrection of His body fulfils His own prophetic word: "Destroy this temple, and in three days I will raise it" (John 2:19). Through all His suffering, the Father remains present with Him, and this accompaniment assures us that God's presence is not absent from our own deepest trials (Rom 8:38–39).

On Good Friday, we are invited to contemplate the profound sacrifice of Christ and the perfect obedience He renders to the Father. His suffering is not in vain but accomplishes our salvation (Isa 53:10–11; Rom 5:8–10). In our own trials, we are called to trust God's sovereign plan and to follow the path of obedience and love, confident that the same Father who raised Christ from the dead is present with us in our suffering.

Closing Prayer

Lord Jesus Christ, I acknowledge that all You endured was for my salvation. Strengthen my faith and grant me the grace to follow Your example of trust, patience, and surrender to the Father. Amen.

Footnotes

1. John 5:19: Emphasizes the ontological and functional unity between the Father and the Son.
2. Hebrews 5:8: Highlights the necessity of Christ's human experience in perfecting His role as High Priest.
3. Exodus 17:1–7: Numbers 20:10–12; 1 Corinthians 10:4, establishes the "Rock" typology where the physical rock provided life-giving water, pointing to Christ.
4. Numbers 20:12: The account of Moses' disobedience at Meribah, contrasting his momentary failure with Christ's perfect endurance.
5. Psalm 69:21 (LXX 68:22): A messianic Psalm describing the suffering of the righteous servant.
6. Psalm 22:1; Matthew 27:46; Mark 15:34: Christ's recitation of the "Psalm of the Cross," which moves from abandonment to final victory.
7. Psalm 31:5; Luke 23:46: The final act of "Tradition," or handing over of His life to the Father.
8. Matthew 27:51; Mark 15:38; Luke 23:45: The physical sign of the end of the Old Covenant's separation between God and man.
9. Hebrews 10:19–20: Theological explanation of the "new and living way" opened through the flesh of Jesus.
10. John 2:19: Christ's self-identification as the true and eternal Temple of God.

HOLY SATURDAY
A DAY OF REFLECTION

Opening Prayer

Almighty God, on this day Your Son lay in the tomb. Judged swiftly by human hands, sentenced, and buried in a single day, He rested in death's shadow. Grant us understanding that You do not will such suffering for Your children and lead us to hope in Your promise of resurrection and eternal life. Amen.

Scripture Reading: John 14:1–6, 27

Reflection

The death that holds Jesus on Good Friday continues through Holy Saturday, until the dawn of Resurrection Day. In this interval, He enters a realm from which no one has returned permanently. It is a time of profound solitude, for even in death, the Lord bears the weight of separation from humanity. However, this darkness is not void of purpose; it is the shadow of His redeeming work.

Jesus' descent into the depths of darkness is not a moment of shame, as some have speculated, but a deliberate journey into the fullness of human suffering and the realm of the dead. As Scripture reminds us in Matthew 12:40, He would lie in the heart of the earth as Jonah did in the belly of the fish.[1] In the quiet of this Sabbath, while creation itself rests, Jesus labors for the liberation of humanity from sin and death.

Psalm 139:12 declares, "Even darkness is not dark to You," affirming that Christ's presence fills even the abyss. In this mysterious work, He proclaims victory over death and anticipates the joy of resurrection. Some scholars note that Christ also preached to the spirits in prison (1 Peter 3:19; 4:6), extending the message of salvation even to those who had not known Him in the flesh. Through Him, the promise of eternal life is secured: "I am the way, the truth, and the life. No one comes to the Father except through Me" (John 14:6).

Thus, Holy Saturday is a day of waiting and hope. The tomb is silent, yet it is pregnant with promise. The darkness is not despair, but preparation for the light that is to come. Even in the stillness, God's redemptive purpose moves unseen, preparing the world for freedom, grace, and eternal communion with Him.

Closing Prayer

Lord Jesus, it is a silent time for the Christian community, as we celebrate the stillness of His Body in the tomb, in preparation for the rising to give us a new life experience. Amen.

Footnotes

1. Matthew 12:40: Referring to the "Sign of Jonah," where Jesus would be in the heart of the earth for three days and three nights.

Easter Day

Christ Is Risen

Easter Day

FREEDOM DAY

Opening Prayer

Lord, Easter reminds us of Your power over all creation, in sickness and in health. Anoint us, we pray, that we may walk in the newness of life that You have given through Your Son Jesus Christ. Amen.

Scripture Reading: Matthew 28:1–10

Reflection

On this glorious day, Jesus Christ bestows upon the world its crowning gift, salvation, which delivers us from sin and death. Through His resurrection, He transforms His disciples from fearful followers into bold witnesses and formally commissions the eleven remaining apostles to proclaim the Gospel to all nations (Matt 28:16–20). The designation Christians for His followers does not appear until later, at Antioch (Acts 11:26), but the resurrection is the decisive event that shapes their identity and mission.

The plan of salvation unfolds through Scripture, beginning in the Old Testament. God promises Abraham a son, despite the barrenness of Sarah's womb and the human plan that led to her servant Hagar bearing Ishmael. From Ishmael's lineage came the Arab peoples, and God also showed faithfulness to Hagar and her son, promising to make Ishmael into a great nation (Gen 21:8–21). The broader table of nations (Gen 10) shows that the Gentile peoples descended from the many sons of Noah.

Isaac, the son of promise, was born when Abraham was one hundred years old, and Sarah was ninety (Gen 17:17;

21:5). Isaac married Rebekah at forty and became the father of Esau and Jacob when he was sixty (Gen 25:20, 26). Through Jacob, whom God renamed Israel, God established the covenant people (Gen 32:28).

The prophet Isaiah foretells the coming of one born of a young woman (almah) who will be called Immanuel (Isa 7:14). The Gospel applies this prophecy to Mary and the virgin birth of Jesus (Matt 1:23). The birthplace of the Messiah in Bethlehem is foretold separately by the prophet Micah (Mic 5:2; cf. Luke 2:6–12). This child, Jesus Christ, is the instrument by which Jews and Gentiles are reconciled under one covenant. As Jeremiah declares, God would establish a new covenant with the peoples of Israel and Judah, distinct from the former (Jer 31:31–34).

On Resurrection Day, Jesus fulfills this promise, bringing all peoples, Jews and Gentiles, together as one reconciled people under Him (2 Cor 5:19). Easter celebrations not only honor the victory won through Jesus' death but also celebrate the freedom offered to all creation through His resurrection. As the culmination of redemptive history, this moment brings to fruition the promises God began to weave in the Old Testament.

Closing Prayer

Christ is risen indeed! He is reigning in our hearts! Hallelujah. Amen.

Footnotes

1. Commissioning of Apostles: Matthew 28:16–20. The Name "Christians": Acts 11:26. Promise to Ishmael: Genesis 21:8–21. Table of Nations: Genesis 10. Birth of Isaac: Genesis 17:17; 21:5.
2. Isaac's Marriage and Sons: Genesis 25:20, 26. Jacob Renamed Israel: Genesis 32:28. Immanuel Prophecy: Isaiah 7:14; Matthew 1:23. Bethlehem Prophecy: Micah 5:2; Luke 2:6–12. New Covenant: Jeremiah 31:31–34.

EASTER MONDAY
A Day of Rest and Rejoicing

Opening Prayer

Lord, You carried us through the forty days of Lenten spiritual discipline. Help us to enter this day with hearts open to joy and reflection, celebrating the gift of Your resurrection and the new life You offer. Amen.

Reflection

While no specific scripture is cited here, the themes of Easter Monday echo Christ's triumph over sin and death, as celebrated in Matthew and throughout the Easter Octave. The day encourages believers to live in the joy and freedom of resurrection.

Easter Monday is a day of reflection and rejoicing, extending the celebration of Easter Sunday into a second day of spiritual renewal. The Church includes Easter Monday within the Easter Octave, a set of eight days that emphasize the significance of Jesus' resurrection. Each day of this Octave continues the joy of Easter Sunday, reminding believers of Christ's victory over death and sin.

Historically, Sundays during Lent were treated as little Easter days, when fasting, kneeling, and acts of penance were forbidden, so that Christians could focus on the resurrection rather than on self-denial. Because Sundays were exempt from fasting, the forty-day Lenten season traditionally yielded approximately thirty-four actual fast days, a practice attested in early patristic sources and canons associated with the Council of Nicaea (AD 325). That same council also ruled on the uniform dating of Easter throughout the Church.

Across cultures and civilizations, Easter Monday has been marked as a day of renewal, often coinciding with the arrival of spring and the awakening of life in nature.

Today, Easter Monday offers an opportunity to rest and enjoy the company of loved ones and friends, free from the burdens of work and routine. It is a day to experience the peace and joy that flow from Christ's triumph, and to reflect on His gift of salvation and the hope it brings.

Closing Prayer

Almighty God, thank You for allowing us to rejoice in Your Son's gift of salvation. May this day be filled with fellowship, joy, and reflection on the life You have restored in us through Christ our Lord. Amen.

Footnotes

1. What is the significance of Easter Monday?: Bible Hub, 2025.
2. Lent: Origin, 2026 Dates & Fasting Rules: History.com, February 13, 2026.
3. Fasting Part 2: Fasting in the Early Church: Fatima.org, July 23, 2020.

Reflections

Personal responses to the journey of Holy Week

THE VEN. ALSON B.H. PERCIVAL, PhD

My Ordination was the commission to
preach and teach the Word;
to keep the joy of Christ alive in all
believers.
To Him be the glory!

Copyright ©

Having worked with Dad, Dr. Percival, on his new book, "A Walk-Through Holy Week," I am proud to offer a layperson's perspective and a synopsis of the Paschal Mystery and the Call to Holy Living. The Paschal Mystery of the Passion, Death, Resurrection and Ascension of Jesus are not just a historical event or a speculative theological concept, but the defining "pattern" of daily life. It is the rhythm of dying to a self-sacrificing ego, selfishness, to rise to a new life of love, hope, and service.

Natasha Percival-Rawlins, MBA

This Holy Week devotional invites readers to walk prayerfully beside Jesus Christ as He sets His face toward Jerusalem, the cross, and the glory of His resurrection. Rooted in Scripture, prayer, and theological reflection, and shaped by the richness of liturgical tradition, the devotional traces the final days of Christ's earthly ministry, from the Temple to Calvary and the victory of the empty tomb. Each day's meditation, from Palm Sunday to Easter Monday, offers spiritual depth, historical insight, and pastoral warmth, illuminating Jesus' obedience, suffering, and sacrificial love. Drawing connections from God's promise to Abraham to the victory of Easter morning, these reflections reveal how God's redemptive purposes prevail even amid human frailty. Calling believers to repentance, deeper communion with God, and renewed commitment to the way of the cross, this devotional transforms Holy Week into more than remembrance. It becomes an invitation to enter the week with reverence, rise with hearts awakened to resurrection joy, and live faithfully in the light of Christ's triumph.

Beverley Bramley-Carnish, Ed.D.

WORKS CITED

The Holy Week devotionals are lightly footnoted. All citations below are drawn from those footnotes.

Colossians 1:15–20 (Scripture Reading, Holy Tuesday) ....HT
John 14:1–6, 27 (Scripture Reading, Holy Saturday)................HS
John 19:31–42 (Scripture Reading, Good Friday)....................GF

Matthew 12:40 — footnote on Sign of Jonah...........................HS
Matthew 21 / Mark 11 — footnote on fig tree and
Bethany/Bethphage...HT
Matt 16:24; Mark 8:34; Luke 9:23; 14:27 — footnote
on cross-bearing logion..HT
2 Cor 5:18–20; Col 1:21–22 — footnote on direction of
reconciliation...HT

INDEX

HOLY WEEK DEVOTIONALS

Abbreviations: HT = Holy Tuesday; GF = Good Friday (Holy Friday); HS = Holy Saturday. References are to those documents, not to page numbers, as each devotional is a brief stand-alone text.

I. SCRIPTURE INDEX

Old Testament

New Testament

Luke
9:23 (cross-bearing logion)..HT
14:27 (cross-bearing logion)..HT
19:29 (departure from Bethphage)..HT
20:45–47 (warning against scribes)...HT
23:45 (tearing of the temple curtain)...GF
23:46 ("Into Thy hands")...GF

John
2:19 ("Destroy this temple")..GF
5:19 ("The Son can do nothing of His own accord")................GF
14:1–6, 27 (Scripture Reading — Holy Saturday)....................HS
14:6 ("I am the way, the truth, and the life").............................HS
19:31–42 (Scripture Reading — Good Friday)..........................GF

Romans
5:8–10 (reconciliation through Christ's death)..........................GF
8:38–39 (nothing separates us from God's love).......................GF

1 Corinthians
10:4 (the Rock — typology)...GF

2 Corinthians
5:18–20 (God reconciling the world)..HT

Galatians
4:4 (born of woman)...HT

Colossians
1:13–15 (Son of God, image of the invisible God)....................HT
1:15–20 (Scripture Reading — Holy Tuesday).........................HT
1:18 (firstborn from the dead)..HT
1:20–22 (cosmic reconciliation)...HT
1:21–22 (you who were once alienated)......................................HT

Hebrews
5:8 ("learned obedience through what He suffered)...............GF
10:19–20 (access to God through Christ's sacrifice)................GF

1 Peter
3:19 (preaching to spirits in prison)...HS
4:6 (gospel preached to the dead)..HS